Axolotl Fact Book for Kids

Fascinating Facts You've Never Heard About the World's Most Interesting Amphibian

© 2023 Ciel Publishing. All rights reserved.

The contents of this book may not be reproduced, duplicated or transmitted without direct written permission from the author.

Legal Notice:
You cannot amend, distribute, sell, use, quote or paraphrase any part of the content of this book without the consent of the author.

Disclaimer Notice:
Please note the information contained in this document is for educational and entertainment purposes only. No warranties of any kind are expressed or implied. Readers acknowledge that the author is not engaging in the rendering of legal, financial, medical or professional advice.

By reading this document, the reader agrees that under no circumstances is the author responsible for any losses, direct or indirect, which are incurred as a result of the use of the information contained within this document, including, but not limited to, errors, omissions, or inaccuracies.

DOWNLOAD YOUR FREE GIFT

Thank you for getting a copy of this book. As a token of my appreciation, I have a special gift for you and your young adventurers called: **"The Axolotl Explorer's Gift Bundle!**

For our young axolotl aficionados, we've prepared a bundle that's as unique and fascinating as these creatures themselves. It's a fun-packed collection that will spark your kid's imagination and turn learning into an epic adventure!

Get this Axolotl Explorer's Gift Bundle for FREE!

WHAT'S INSIDE?

- Axolotl Fact Book for Kids Audiobook

- Axolotl Fact Sheets and Templates

- Axolotl Care Sheet

- Axolotl Coloring Pages

- Axolotl Color by Number

- How To Draw Axolotl

Eager to dive deeper into the axolotl universe? Just scan the QR code to get your Axolotl Explorer's Gift Bundle and keep the waves of fun rolling!

Let's jump into the adventure - where learning about these awesome animals is as cool as discovering buried treasure!

AXOLOTL

[ak-suh-lo-tl]

a neotenic salamander with extraordinary regenerative abilities

TABLE OF CONTENTS

INTRODUCTION

Axolotls (yes, that is exactly their name! And it's pronounced ak-suh-lo-tl) are adorable little amphibians that live in the freshwaters and lakes of Mexico. Unlike other amphibians, Axolotls do not go through metamorphosis, which means they do not grow limbs and lungs that would help them walk on land. So, they spend their entire lives underwater and retain their youthful looks. Though they originate from Mexico, they've been brought to other countries by explorers who were fascinated by the creatures.

Axolotls are essentially salamanders. Since they spend their whole lives underwater, they have gills, webbed feet, and a tail for swimming. Their colors vary from brownish-green to pink.

The pink ones are the ones we usually see a lot. Their mouths are permanently turned up into a smile.

The Axolotl gets its name from the Aztec god of fire and lightning, Xolotl. Xolotl disguised himself as an amphibian so he can escape his enemies.

Whether you're discovering Axolotls for the first time or are planning to keep them as pets, this book will help you know all about these special creatures. Though they do not require a lot of food and fun, and it's easy to care for them, it's still important to know how to look after them properly. Axolotls may require cold-water tanks and their food requirements need to be studied properly. After all, such special pets need special care.

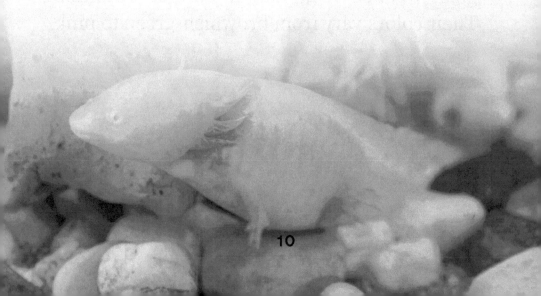

CHAPTER ONE:
All About Axolotls

Axolotls are so popular they can be found in homes and aquariums everywhere in the world. They're so cute that it's natural for people to want to own one. Axolotls bred in captivity live up to fifteen long years, but the ones in the wild only live for five to six years.

You don't normally find Axolotls in any pet shop. It is quite illegal to keep them as pets in certain states of the US like California, Maine, New Jersey, Washington DC, and Virginia. New Mexico and Hawaii need you to have a special permit for keeping Axolotls. It is not allowed to keep them in certain states of Canada as well.

The reason is that if Axolotls that are raised at home are released into the wild, they could pose threats to the environment. They would become harmful to the wild Axolotls.

So if you buy an Axolotl as a pet, it is important to make sure they are from a trusted breeder.

PHYSICAL DESCRIPTION

Axolotls are "neotenic," which means they retain the features they had as larvae. As such, they look like babies their entire lives. They're closely related to the Tiger Salamander. Axolotls have feathery gills on their heads, a dorsal fin running along their body, a tail, and webbed feet for swimming underwater. They range in a variety of colors.

Their mouths are permanently shaped like a smile. They keep their mouths open for a while after feeding, and it looks like they're always smiling. In the wild, they're usually brownish-green or black with gold specks. The albino ones, or the bright pink ones we are familiar with, are more common in captivity.

Axolotls can grow up to 15-45 cm in length. They are easy to recognize, as males have broad skulls

and do not have eyelids and their tails are much longer than the females. The females have rounder, more swollen bodies. It is more common to find Axolotls in their albino forms because of their transparent skin. They can move at speeds of up to 10 miles per hour (15 kilometers per hour). They have a three-chambered heart.

These creatures are small and only weigh up to 50-250 grams. Much like other amphibians, reptiles, and fishes, Axolotls can regrow missing limbs. But that's not all they can regrow. They can also regrow missing jaws, spinal cords, skin, ovary, and lung tissue. Even parts of their hearts and brains! They retain this ability throughout their lives. It's almost like a superpower. They can also change their colors slightly to adapt to their surroundings.

Because of this special ability, Axolotls can also be found in research laboratories where scientists study them closely.

Since they can regenerate missing parts right down to the bones, muscles, and skins, scientists hope to someday be able to apply these abilities to humans and save lives.

DID YOU KNOW?

The feathery growth at the side of Axolotls' heads are gills. They breathe through them.

NATURAL HABITAT

Axolotls originate in Central Mexico. Before they used to live across the region's lakes and wetlands, but now, they can only be found at Lake Xochimilco (pronounced So-Chee-Mil-Koh) in Mexico City. Their former home, Lake Chalco, had been drained to avoid flooding, until there was nothing left but canals and waterways. The loss of habitat caused the scarcity of Axolotls along with the entry of predators like carp and tilapia (Georgia State University & Young Harris College, 2022).

The water temperature at Lake Xochimilco is about 20 degrees Celsius, and Axolotls have adapted to this climate. However, the invasive fish often fight with Axolotls for food. They even eat them, causing the number of Axolotls to decline. The decline in number is also caused by Mexico's continuously developing city. As more and more buildings come up, the natural environment is getting damaged. Water pollution is yet another factor in the decrease in their numbers.

Another reason why they are reducing in number is because they are a delicacy in Mexico. They are considered as food and this does a huge harm to their existence. Awareness is being raised about them so they can be saved.

Despite there being a large number of these creatures in captivity, they are still critically endangered.

Why is their decline a troubling thing?

There are less than 1,000 Axolotls left in the wild.

They are special, unusual amphibians. They're highly important to scientists as they're studied closely and frequently. Their regenerative abilities have fascinated researchers for years, who believe that humans have a lot to learn from the Axolotls. They believe the abilities can be valuable in medicine and perhaps can save humans from certain diseases.

Therefore, conservation efforts are being made to restore the Axolotls' habitats. That includes raising the water levels of Lake Xochimilco and reducing the number of invasive fish that might harm them.

LIFE CYCLE

Axolotls live up to 15 years in captivity, and only up to five or six years in the wild. But if they're taken good care of, then they can last up to 20 years in captivity. The huge difference in lifespan is because of the dangers of their natural habitats. In the wild, Axolotls are prone to illnesses and are prey to predators. The harmful effects of the destruction of their habitats also add to the decrease in their lifespan.

Axolotls live underwater all their lives as their lungs don't fully develop to help them walk on land. They mostly use their gills, but sometimes, they use their lungs to take in air from the water's surface.

They even breed underwater. Their breeding season starts in spring, from March to June. Axolotls mate when they reach six months of age, and their mating ritual consists of a kind of "waltz." They dance around the water. Females can lay up to 1000 eggs at one time, and this breeding process may repeat if they wish. The females have the ability to reproduce more than once, restarting the breeding process after each one.

The eggs hatch after two weeks, and the Axolotls are off on their own. There is no parental care. The larvae reach maturity after six months and are considered fully grown when they're one-year-old.

The most common factors that lead to the death of Axolotls are:

Predators - Axolotls can't defend themselves. They don't have many defensive features and are thus easy targets for predators. Even bigger axolotls feed on smaller axolotls, as a way of natural selection.

Illnesses - Axolotls are prone to fluid build-ups, tumors, bacteria, fungi, and parasites. Some of their illnesses are also caused by inbreeding, which is one of the many causes of their decline in numbers. This inbreeding is also sadly leading to their extinction.

Poor Care - Axolotls can become ill due to improper care. Being so fragile, they require large tanks and cold waters. Dirty tanks, poor filtration, or injuries from the poor set-up of tanks can cause death to these creatures. Although Axolotls adapt well in comparison to other fish, they still require good care and environment. (Hall, 2021)

DID YOU KNOW?

Axolotls are the top predators in their natural habitats? Just because they have cute baby faces, doesn't mean they're not tough. They eat other smaller fishes, insects, worms, and much more!

CHAPTER TWO:
Axolotl Diets

Now that we know that Axolotls require special care and environment, it's important to note the kind of foods they eat. While some types of foods can be good for them, others might be harmful or even hinder their growth. It's good to study their feeding habits and their diet before planning to keep one as a pet.

FEEDING HABITS

Axolotls are essentially carnivores. They eat small fish, crustaceans, mollusks, and insects. While in captivity, they eat beef liver, earthworms, fish pellets, and much more. It all depends on what suits them. Inadequate food can cause them to fall ill or become aggressive towards other Axolotls if you're planning on keeping more than one.

Axolotls eat by sucking their food, almost like a vacuum cleaner. They also suck in gravel along with their food to help them digest it. Taking in the gravel also helps to control how they float about in the water. They don't have teeth the way we do, where we can bite and tear our food. Their teeth are somewhat cone-like and only help with gripping food as it comes in.

So if you're feeding them worms, for example, small worms would be easier for them to eat, rather than large ones. Axolotls only go for such foods that fit into their mouths, otherwise, they simply give up.

Fish pellets work best on Axolotls. You may give them live food such as earthworms, bloodworms, and brine shrimp, but be very careful not to give them too much, or else they can spread parasites and diseases. Kind of like how you get a tummy ache when you have too much candy. Daphnia is another great option. It's a kind of crustacean, also known as a water flea.

Wild Axolotls have a more varied diet. They feed on mosquitoes, snails, worms, tadpoles, and other small aquatic animals.

The amount of food they eat depends on their life cycle. Babies require more food and they eat frequently. As they grow a bit older, they feed once or twice a day. Make sure to feed them separately from other fish.

FAVORITE FOODS

EARTHWORMS

The diets of Axolotls are largely made up of protein, anywhere from 30 to 60 percent. It's straightforward, but at the same time, lots of foods might contain parasites. Therefore, it's important to keep watch on the food you give them. The most popular recommendation for food would be Nightcrawlers, which are large earthworms. They're easy to find and are an absolute favorite of the Axolotls. You would often find them munching on these earthworms. Of course, there are many varieties of these earthworms. Some of them are:

Red Wigglers: Red Wigglers are smaller than other types of nightcrawlers, and they're easy for Axolotls to eat without being cut up to pieces. The only problem is that these earthworms excrete a foul substance, because of which Axolotls avoid eating them. And they're especially not suitable for babies.

Black Worms: These worms are great for young Axolotls. They are much smaller and their nutritional content is similar to the other earthworms, but it would require a lot of Black Worms to feed an adult Axolotl. The biggest problem with these types of worms is that they make quite a mess in the tank, which would need regular cleaning.

Bloodworms: Another favorite of Axolotls. These worms are a popular choice among owners, but unlike the other worms, bloodworms aren't nutritionally healthy. So, it's recommended to give these as an occasional treat for young or adult Axolotls. They come freeze-dried, so it's easier to store them. These worms, like Black Worms, also tend to make a mess. They develop fungus if they're kept in the tank for too long.

DAPHNIAS

Another favorite of pet owners is Daphnias. Daphnias are planktonic crustaceans, also called water fleas. They're rich in fatty acids and lipids, but they don't provide a lot of nutrition to your Axolotls. Instead, they leave them constantly hungry and wanting more. In addition, Daphnias also spread parasites and diseases, so it's important to make sure you know where you're buying them from. It's always better to buy your pet supplies from stores that have high-quality products or you could also artificially grow Daphnias at home on your own.

PELLETS

If you feel icky about feeding your cute little amphibians live food, then a great alternative would be to feed them pellets. Salmon pellets are a good choice. Make sure to buy pellets that sink in the water, so Axolotls are able to suck them into their mouths. For younger Axolotls, small pellets work better. The pellets need to be soft so they can easily grab them with their mouths. You can use rounded forceps to drop the pellets near their mouths.

BRINE SHRIMP

One of the most nutritious choices would be Brine Shrimp. These can also be artificially grown at home, just like Daphnias. However, it can be quite hard for baby Brine Shrimp to reach the mouths of your Axolotls, so it's better to use a Turkey Baster syringe. It's a kind of long tube that's used to inject food and other things. You can use these to place the food closer to the Axolotl's mouths so they can take it in. But be sure to clean up any remaining Brine Shrimps or they can make the water cloudy and dirty up the tank.

GHOST SHRIMP

Ghost Shrimps are an uncommon choice for a snack. They don't carry diseases and they even help with cleaning out the tank by eating up leftover food. They have soft shells which make them easy for Axolotls to eat. Perhaps the only downside to Ghost Shrimps is that they're expensive. Guppies, on the other hand, are another alternative.

Bonus fact: Chopped mosquito larvae can be fed to Axolotl larvae that have grown to two centimeters.

FOODS TO AVOID

Although Axolotls eat crustaceans, any food with a hard shell will not digest easily, so make sure to give them foods that are soft and easy to digest. Be mindful of treats and snacks, as these aren't nutritious and you need to watch out for their nutrition. Do not ever feed them human food. It's bad for them! Do not feed them mealworms. Mealworms contain a fibrous substance called chitin, which makes up for the hard exoskeletons. And as mentioned above, giving anything hard to the Axolotls can harm their health.

Feeding them a varied diet helps them stay healthy. Feeding them only one kind of food will either not provide them with proper nutrition or might lead to their deaths.

FEEDING SCHEDULE

So now that we know what kinds of foods Axolotls eat, how often do you need to feed them?

Baby Axolotls eat frequently, so you need to feed them every day. Adult Axolotls eat twice or thrice a week and can go up to 14 days without eating. Brine shrimps, as mentioned above, are the best foods to start with when you're first feeding them. Mosquito larvae are another great starter food. You should always feed the Axolotls in moderation since feeding them too much causes them to fall sick.

Make sure the food you give them sinks to the bottom of the tank since they tend to stay there. You can use tweezers or Turkey Baster syringes to drop the food in the water close by. This helps keep the tank clean as well.

Good thing these little creatures know exactly when their tummy is full. They will know when to stop eating.

It's best to turn off the aquarium pump before feeding so no food particles get distributed around the aquarium.

CHAPTER THREE:
Axolotl Behavior

Aside from their interesting regenerative abilities, Axolotls are mostly inactive. They simply lie in one place for the most part, and when they do move about, it's quite slow. Bright lights drive them into hiding. They usually hide under rocks or between underwater plants.

SOCIAL HABITS

Axolotls are solitary creatures. They're not that active throughout the day, but are more active during the night. They have soft, permeable skin, so it's not recommended to touch them as this might damage their skin.

Axolotls aren't essentially social animals. They're loners by nature and enjoy being alone. So, if you're keeping one as a pet, you don't have to worry about whether they would be alone or might need company. It's not necessary to have another Axolotl, but if you do adopt another one, they may live in peace with each other but may not necessarily like each other. That said, if you plan on having two of them, then make sure it's a male and a female. Adults are better off with adults. If you have a baby Axolotl with an adult, chances are the adult might eat the baby.

They should not be kept in the same tank with other pet fishes as these creatures because Axolotls tend to eat any other kind of pet fish. They are not sociable at all.

TERRITORIAL BEHAVIOR

Axolotls aren't normally aggressive, but they can be while protecting their territory. Otherwise, they're somewhat of a recluse. But when they do get aggressive, they can bite each other's gills, tails, and feet off.

They usually become aggressive when they're forced to share a tank with another Axolotl.

To humans, Axolotls are quite safe. They don't bite you unless, of course, you provoke them. But for the most part, they tend to enjoy human interaction. Just don't put your finger too close to their mouths.

COMMUNICATION

It is said that Axolotls recognize their owners and swim up to them to nuzzle or to receive a gentle pat. A lot of pet owners report the same, but this behavior might simply be the Axolotl thinking you have a treat to give them.

During mating, Axolotls communicate with visual and chemical cues. There isn't a lot of communication outside of mating. They can also detect electrical fields and use their vision to perceive their environment and detect prey (Majchrzak, n.d.).

Although a lot of videos out there show Axolotls "barking," these creatures cannot talk or make any sort of sound. They're silent as they don't have vocal cords. But they can produce sounds by gulping the air off the surface of the water and contracting their muscles. This creates barking and squeaking sounds.

Their main communication is by leaving chemical trails. But the sounds they make might not be to communicate. It's more unintentional. They are essentially deaf and have poor vision, and move through the water by sensing vibrations. As such, they don't have any mating calls.

DID YOU KNOW?

When Axolotls mate, they get into a kind of dance with the females, like a waltz! They lead the females around the water while breeding.

CHAPTER FOUR:
Axolotl Care

As mentioned earlier, Axolotls require special care and a certain kind of environment. They don't require company and prefer to be alone. That doesn't mean you can't own a second Axolotl, but be careful when you decide to adopt more than one. They might not like each other's company. Or at the very least, make sure the second Axolotl is of the opposite gender.

TANK SETUP

Young Axolotls can be cannibalistic—meaning they could eat each other. It's better to keep them in separate, smaller tanks. Adults should be kept in larger tanks with cold water. You can have more than one adult Axolotl, but you need to keep a close watch on them to prevent any fighting. Do not keep adults and babies together, as the adults might eat the babies.

The right tank size for a young Axolotl would be 10 gallons. For an adult, it is 20 gallons with at least six inches of swimming space. If you plan on keeping a second adult, then 40 gallons is preferable. The bigger the aquarium, the better for them. The tank should have a glass top so the creatures don't jump out of the aquarium.

The bodies of Axolotls are made up of mainly cartilage and are extremely delicate, so don't handle them unless absolutely necessary. If you must take them out of the tank, then use a soft, fine mesh net so their limbs don't get trapped.

Use low lighting for the tank. Axolotls get disturbed if the lights are too bright and they hide away in a dark place. Since they're nocturnal creatures, you can give them a hiding spot, like an aquarium castle.

The floor of the aquarium can have gravel, but make sure the gravel is not too small. If the gravel is too small, they might accidentally ingest it. It needs to be bigger than the Axolotl's head.

There need to be more hiding places for them so they can hide during the daylight. This could be a stack of rocks or hollow ceramic rocks, but make sure everything in the tank is smooth and there are absolutely no sharp edges that might harm them. Their extremely sensitive skin can easily get injured otherwise. All sharp edges would be avoided.

WATER QUALITY

Tap water should be treated with an aquarium water conditioner to remove chemicals like chlorine and chloramines. If you don't plan on using a filtered tank, then you would need to change the water regularly. About 20 percent of it. Don't change the entire water as that would change its chemistry and stress out Axolotls.

Make sure the pH level of the water is 7.4 to 7.6. You can get a water testing kit to check the level.

Some owners find filtered tanks much easier to clean. If you are using a filtered tank, make sure the filtration rate is slow. If the filtration is high, it can cause strong currents, which may also stress out the Axolotls. You only need to clean 20 percent of the tank every week.

You can use sponge filters. Their flow is lesser compared to other pumps and filters.

TEMPERATURE REQUIREMENTS

Axolotls cannot survive in warmer waters. This might be strange since they live in Mexico, and temperatures can rise there. But the lakes at which Axolotls reside are at higher altitudes, where the temperature is a lot cooler than at lower altitudes. Therefore, they've adapted to the cooler temperatures. Warm waters stress them out and they may not survive.

The water temperature of your tank must be at that level, anywhere between 14 degrees Celsius to 20 degrees Celsius and no more than 24 degrees Celsius. There should be plenty of oxygen in the tank, as that could make a lot of difference.

CLEANING AND MAINTENANCE

REMOVING WATER

While cleaning, you need to remove 20 to 25 percent of the water. Make sure not to remove more than that or you might disrupt the nitrogen cycle. Axolotls don't need to be removed from the tank before cleaning, but just make sure you don't disturb them. You can use a tube called a "siphon" to clean debris and waste food from the tank, or even a Turkey Baster syringe.

SCRUBBING

To remove algae from the tank, use an aquarium sponge brush. The brush can be used to clean other surfaces inside the tank. If you have any artificial plants and decorations, then it's best to take them out and clean them with disinfected water. Have a bucket of disinfected water set aside for this.

If you have a sponge filter, then clean this with the disinfected water too. If your tank filter has any cartridges, you can clean them with this water as well, but make sure you don't remove the cartridges all at once. Remove them one at a time for cleaning.

REARRANGE EVERYTHING

Axolotls tend to move things around in the tank. If you find the plants, decorations, and rocks in different places, don't be surprised. These cute little creatures can be quite the explorers. Before you fill the tank up, make sure to put everything back where it was.

FILL THE TANK BACK UP

Before you fill the tank with water again, it's important to remember to use a water conditioner that's safe for Axolotls. You can use a hose to fill the tank easier and then add the water conditioner. Just make sure the temperature of the water remains the same before you put the Axolotls in. Do not use cooler or warmer water.

Some pointers to remember:

- ❑ Use a tube to remove waste and debris.
- ❑ Do not leave excess food in the tank after you've fed the Axolotls.
- ❑ Use a water testing kit to test the water to make sure it's nice and safe for them.

TIPS FOR BREEDING AXOLOTL

If you plan on keeping a male and a female Axolotl with the intention to breed, make sure you study their life cycle and mating seasons. Breeding season usually takes place in spring, from March to June. Females lay anywhere from 300 to 1000 eggs.

It takes five months to several years for Axolotls to reach maturity, depending on the quality of food and care, and the condition of their environment. Males take around six months to reach maturity. Females take a little longer.

According to Clare (n.d.), it's advised to breed Axolotls once they've reached at least 18 months of age, where they've reached their full size and maturity. You'll know when a female is ready to breed because their body will look rounder towards the end when you see them from above. Males can be bred at a much earlier stage than females because the breeding doesn't put a lot of strain on their bodies. But with females, it's better to wait until they're fully mature because they lay over 1000 eggs and this can strain their bodies.

Females can breed more than once a year. Once they lay eggs the first time, they can then lay more eggs. This might cause them to fall ill unless they're taken care of properly. Once the female has laid eggs the first time, keep them away from the males for at least a month so they can recover.

In order to encourage breeding between them, their tanks need to be kept away from sunlight, but somewhere where there's a temperature change. The change in temperature, when it drops, and the water gets colder, usually stimulates the males, and the females become more receptive.

While breeding, it's good to have plastic plants in the tank, since they don't wither, and they can serve as a nest where the females can lay eggs on their leaves. For the males, having some rough stones at the bottom of the tank can provide a surface where they can leave their spermatophores for the females to carry and fertilize.

Males usually shake their tails vigorously, leading the female around the tank in a kind of "waltz," after which they leave cone-shaped masses called **spermatophores**, which the females pick up into their cloacas and fertilize in their bodies.

It will take a few hours to two days for the female to start laying the eggs one by one, and she usually lays them on the leaves of plants. If there are no plants in the tank, then she will find a rock, a pipe, or any other surface to where she can attach the eggs. Once she has laid all the eggs, it's best to remove her from the male for a while, as mentioned above.

The eggs are 2mm in diameter and contain an embryo. They are covered in jelly. They take about 17 days to hatch. Remove them from the tank after they've been laid because Axolotls do have the tendency to eat their eggs sometimes! It's better to keep the eggs in a separate tank.

Hatching the eggs would depend on the temperature. The temperature should be just right, about 25 degree Celsius. You can place an air stone at one end of the tank. Plenty of oxygen will help them hatch.

Newly hatched Axolotls do not eat immediately. After 48 hours, you can feed them tiny pieces of live food in large quantities because they eat a lot.

It's important to feed young larvae at least once or twice per day, otherwise they tend to bite each other! You may see them with missing limbs if this happens, so it's better to cater to their feeding regularly. Although Axolotls are known to regenerate missing limbs, it's better to avoid their cannibal tendencies entirely.

It takes about nine days for the larvae to form the front legs and about three weeks to form the hind legs. Once the front legs are formed, they actively hunt for food. They develop lungs at the same time as their hind legs. Once they grow hind legs, you can cut up earthworms into small pieces and feed them.

Once they grow, their cannibalistic tendencies disappear. Pay attention to what the adult Axolotls like to eat. Have a big tank and plenty of space for them to move about.

DID YOU KNOW?

Axolotls are an endangered species?
There are not many left in the wild.
Efforts are being made to restore
their natural homes and increase
their numbers.

CHAPTER FIVE:
Axolotl Health

Sometimes Axolotls fall ill. The cause can be anything. They need a lot of care to make sure their illnesses do not result in death. There are signs and symptoms to help you find out if your little creature is not doing so well.

COMMON HEALTH PROBLEMS

WATER QUALITY AND TEMPERATURE CHANGES

Axolotls can fall sick quicker when they're stressed. The most common reason is a strong water flow in the tank. If the filter is too forceful, this can stress them out. Other reasons would be water changes, sudden changes in temperature, untreated water, parasites, and even other fish that don't belong in the same tank as the Axolotls. A build-up of Ammonia and Nitrite from poor filtration can also harm them and may result in their deaths.

GENETICS

One other health problem is fluid build-up and tumors. Sometimes these are caused by genetics and there's not a lot you can do about it. In these times, as sad as it is, it's simply best to let nature take control and decide. But do not try to treat any genetic illness yourself. If your Axolotl has a fluid build-up, best take it to a vet and let them handle it. The fluid build-up is caused by heart damage, kidney problems, lack of nutrition, and old age. In these cases, nothing can be done and the fluids tend to build up each time.

NUTRITIONAL PROBLEMS

Bad nutrition can lead to certain health problems as well. Axolotls can't handle foods with high fat and oil content. White worms have high-fat content. Mealworms are low in calcium, and these aren't even recommended for Axolotls, since they have a hard shell. On occasions, though, you may give them mealworms as a snack, but make sure you crush their jaws before feeding them to Axolotls so they don't harm them internally. If nutrition is causing your pet to fall ill, then change its diet immediately and give them different kinds of foods. A lack of proper nutrition can cause Axolotls to develop a bacterial or fungal disease.

INJURIES

If an Axolotl loses a limb or a gill, this usually solves itself, since it can regenerate. As long as it doesn't get infected and as long as the Axolotl is left on its own to heal in clean, cool water. To prevent infection, you can add a teaspoon of salt to two liters of water. Axolotls heal faster at lower temperatures, so the water can be set to 15 degrees to help them heal. They recover fast when they're well-fed and kept in good, cool conditions.

EXCESSIVE FLOATING

Excessive floating is caused by gas buildup in the stomachs of Axolotls. This could be caused by bad water quality, indigestion, tank water being too warm, constipation, ingestion of gravel, and irregular feeding schedules. When you find your Axolotl floating about the water and cannot get to the bottom, then take it out and put it in a container with an air stone and a small quantity of water so the Axolotl can rest on the ground until it deflates.

Until then, check the ammonia and nitrate levels in your tank and make sure they're at a minimum.

If your Axolotl doesn't deflate even after two days, best to take it to a vet.

FUNGAL INFECTION (MYCOSIS)

Mycosis is a type of fungus that looks like a soft, white, fluffy, cotton-like formation that appears on an Axolotl. It is said that salt baths help kill the fungus. Fungi thrive in cold water, which is bad news, since we keep Axolotls in cold water.

Salt might temporarily get rid of the fungus, but there's a chance that fungi might return, and too much salt might damage your sensitive Axolotl. A tea bath might work. There are medications, but be careful about what medicine you give to your Axolotl. The medicine might be harmful to them and might do more bad than good.

Do not try to pull the fungus from their bodies. Whatever treatment you use, it will take at least 1-2 weeks for the problem to resolve. To be safe, you can always take them to a vet.

This infection is caused by poor water quality, and poor maintenance of the tank. When you fail to clean up waste from the tank, fungi tend to grow. Fungus can also form from an injury or when bitten by another Axolotl.

PARASITES

Parasites are caused by live food. Certain foods you give to your Axolotl might spread parasites and cause them to fall ill. Keep an eye on the food you give them. Parasites can be removed by giving your Axolotl a salt bath. Sometimes even leeches can stick onto them. You can simply soak your Axolotl in a salt bath until the leech comes off. Do not try to pull the leech away. It will only hurt the Axolotl even more.

SIGNS OF ILLNESS

Some of the signs and symptoms of a sick Axolotl are:

- ❑ Folded tails or gill - This is caused by stress, maybe strong water flow

- ❑ Redness on skin or flaky skin - you see red marks or it seems like their skin is falling off

- ❑ Their gills deteriorate

- ❑ Scratching frequently

- ❑ White cottony growth on gills or body (fungus)

- ❑ Cuts and scratches on gills, limbs, or fin (any wound or injury can cause them to catch an infection)

- ❑ They don't eat properly (Mostly caused by parasites)

- ❑ They constantly float at the surface of the water

- ❑ Swelling on the head, limbs, or body

- ❑ If the gravel in the tank is small enough for them to eat, then it could upset their stomachs and cause blockage

There aren't a lot of guides and tips on how to treat them when signs of an illness occur, so it's best to take some preventive measures.

PREVENTIVE MEASURES

You know what they say, prevention is better than cure. You can prevent your little creature from falling sick and avoid a lot of problems.

❑ When you see bent or folded gills or tails in your Axolotl, it could be because of stress or because the water flow is too strong. To prevent this, change the water flow, make sure you have proper plants and rocks in your tank (ones that don't harm them), and make sure the water is nice and cool, and clean.

❑ Skin problems can be prevented by making sure the water is clean and is being cleaned regularly. You can use salt baths if your Axolotl is having any skin problems, but make sure not to use too much salt as this can harm their very sensitive skins.

❑ If your Axolotl has been injured, then carefully take it out of the tank with a soft mesh net and put it in a tea bath. It will help it to heal. Do not touch or carry them with your hands as this might damage their skin. Always use a soft net.

❑ If your Axolotl is floating near the surface of the water, this could be a gas problem in their tummies. Gently remove the Axolotl and place it in a container with an air stone and just enough water to cover its body so it can lie on the floor and relax until it deflates. You will need to cover them with a towel and keep them in the fridge. Make sure to check and clean the waste in the container now and then. This is called fridging treatment. To prevent floating altogether, make sure there is plenty of oxygen in the water.

❑ Sometimes you see your Axolotl not eating properly. In this case, check the water conditions and keep a constant watch on them. You may need to use the fridging treatment if they have any tummy problems.

❑ If they have swelling on their head, limbs, or body, then it's best to take them to a vet.

Proper care, good, clean, and cool water, the correct temperature, good food and nutrition, and regular cleaning are the most important points to remember, in order to prevent any illnesses.

REGENERATIVE ABILITIES

Did you know: Axolotls are resistant to cancer?

Yes, Axolotls are remarkable creatures! They can not only regrow limbs, but parts of their brains and organs. And they show an amazing resistance to cancer. The genes that help them grow limbs back are the same in humans as well, which is why scientists and researchers are studying this curious creature closely. They hope to learn about how these creatures regenerate so they can use the same secret to help humans who are injured or suffering diseases, to help them regenerate and heal the same way Axolotls can.

This could help in medical research and can save lives, hopefully, if all goes well. Humans suffer injuries where they lose limbs. We might not be able to regrow our limbs as remarkably as Axolotls do, but at least learning about their abilities might help us make life-saving discoveries.

It is said that during the regrowth process, Axolotls regrow their limbs fully by the fifth time. It is an amazing thing that they can even regrow tissues in their body, their organs, and their brains. Even their skins. No wonder scientists are so curious and fascinated by them!

Of course, other salamanders and amphibians have regenerative abilities too, but none can do it like the Axolotls.

BONUS FACT: IMPORTANCE OF AXOLOTLS IN MYTHOLOGY

We know the Axolotl derived its name from Xolotl, the god of fire and lightning. Xolotl had a brother with whom he used to go to the underworld and take bones back to the light. He got mixed up in a lot of problems with the other gods and was afraid he might get banished or lose his life, so he went underwater and turned himself into an Axolotl to try and escape them.

The name Axolotl means "water monster." They were revered by the ancient Aztecs. They believed it was a reincarnation of Xolotl, because of its regenerative powers. They also believed it resembled the lake that provided them with water, and it is food given to them by this lake. They saw the Axolotls as a deity.

In Aztec culture, the Axolotl is mentioned in the Florentine Codex, which is an ancient manuscript in book form. After that, the Axolotl made an appearance in the book of natural history in 1615. Even though the creature had been mentioned a long time ago, it took 200 years to give it its official scientific name.

FUN ACTIVITIES

SALAMANDER-IFFIC COLORING 1

Bring this adorable axolotl to life
with your favorite colors!

SALAMANDER-IFFIC COLORING 2
Bring this adorable axolotl to life
with your favorite colors!

COPYCAT CHALLENGE
Copy the axolotl on the left
and draw it on the next page.

YOUR TURN!
Get creative and draw your own axolotl
in the space provided below.

	A	B	C	D	E	F
1						
2						
3						
4						
5						
6						
7						

AXOLOTL COLOR CRAZE 1
Match numbers with colors
a picture!

(1) pink   (3) red   (5) violet   (7) green

(2) orange   (4) blue   (6) yellow

AXOLOTL COLOR CRAZE 2
Match numbers with colors
a picture!

1 pink   3 yellow   5 blue

2 orange   4 red

AXOLOTL-LUJAH!
Follow the steps provided to
draw your own axolotl!

YOUR TURN!

Get creative and draw your own axolotl in the space provided below.

AXOLOTL ADVENTURE
Find the hidden words related to axolotls in the puzzle below.

```
F  N  E  Y  E  L  S  U  J  L  M
C  W  L  L  P  R  V  P  U  O  D
I  S  I  P  C  P  A  M  M  V  F
T  G  N  Y  Y  H  A  W  P  E  Q
A  R  E  F  B  N  I  H  Y  L  K
U  C  V  H  E  L  N  L  G  Y  J
Q  D  U  O  D  F  R  I  L  L  Y
A  N  J  D  R  I  E  W  R  Y  Y
N  Y  L  G  G  I  W  N  R  G  M
S  M  I  L  I  N  G  J  V  K  F
L  A  C  I  G  A  M  F  I  V  J
```

Agile   Aquatic   Chilly
Frilly   Grinny   Happy
Jumpy   Juvenile   Lovely
Magical   Smiling   Weird
             Wild
             Wiggly

AXOLOTL WORD WIZARD
Using the letters from the word 'axolotl',
create as many words as you can.

AXOLOTL

Words must be three letters or more,
and proper nouns are not allowed.

_____ _____ _____

_____ _____ _____

_____ _____ _____

_____ _____ _____

_____ _____ _____

_____ _____ _____

73

SALAMANDER-IFFIC COLORING 3
Bring this adorable axolotl to life
with your favorite colors!

ANSWER KEY
Unlock the secrets and reveal
the solutions with the mighty answer key.

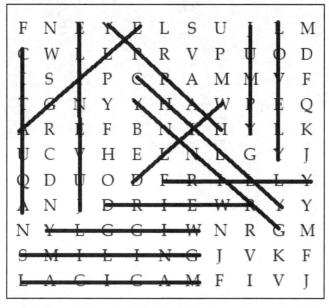

AXOLOTL ADVENTURE PAGE 70

Sample answers:

all	oat	too
alt	tax	alto
lat	atoll	loot
lax	taxol	tool
loo		toll
lot		allot

AXOLOTL WORD WIZARD PAGE 71

CONCLUSION

Axolotls are certainly the cutest, most curious and peculiar creatures. It's no wonder that people want to keep them as pets. They make great pets too but just need a lot of special care and nutrition. Their skin can be extremely delicate, so it is better to not touch or hold them unless it is necessary. It is better to use a fine mesh net if you need to take them out of a tank. It's easy for them to fall sick or get injured, but there are ways to prevent this by making sure they're kept in a good environment with good food and good water conditions.

If they are too sick, then it is best to take them to a vet who knows how to treat exotic animals.

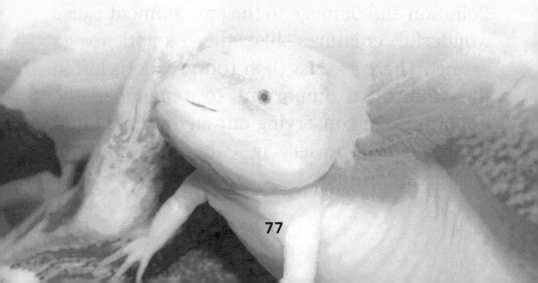

Other than the Axolotls which are now kept at homes, the number of wild Axolotls in their natural habitats is very less. They now mostly live in the lakes of Xochimilco of Mexico, but because of pollution, waste, and predators, they are decreasing in numbers. They are now critically endangered species. Efforts are being made to restore their natural homes and increase their numbers.

These cute little amphibians were very important to the ancient Aztecs. They were considered deities. And even today, they are vital to science and research. They could help in curing illnesses and other injuries in human beings once scientists learn the secret behind their super healing and regrowing powers.

Imagine what it would be like if we were able to regrow missing limbs!

Pollution and damage to the environment cause wonderful creatures like the Axolotl to go extinct. There are less than 1000 Axolotls left in the wild. It is important to remember the importance of conserving our environment and water and preserving these wonderful creatures.

THANK YOU

Thank you for taking the time to read my book about axolotls. I hope you enjoyed learning about these amazing creatures as much as I enjoyed writing about them.

By learning about axolotls, you have taken an important step in understanding and appreciating the natural world around us. I encourage you to continue exploring and learning about other fascinating animals and plants.

If you've enjoyed this book, please leave a positive review on the product page. Your feedback is important to me, and it helps other readers decide if this book is right for them.

Thank you again for your support, and I wish you all the best in your future explorations!

REFERENCES

American Tarantula & Animals. (2022, August 1). *What Do Axolotls Eat?(Diet, Care & Feeding Tips).* https://www.atshq.org/what-do-axolotls-eat/

Bernard, R. (2023). *Axolotl Care Guide For Beginners: A Comprehensive Beginner's Guide On How To Care, Feed, Train, Groom, Health, House Axolotl.* In Google Books. https://www.google.ae/books/edition/AXOLOTL_CARE_GUIDE_FOR_BEGINNERS/5S2yEAAAQBAJ?hl=en&gbpv=1&dq=axolotls%20behavior&pg=PT6&printsec=frontcover

Blue Reef Aquarium. (2020, October 30). *What Is An Axolotl And Their Habitat?* | Blue Reef Aquarium Portsmouth. https://www.bluereefaquarium.co.uk/portsmouth/blog/education/what-is-an-axolotl-and-why-are-they-endangered/#:~:text=The%20axolotl%20is%20native%20only

Brown, L. (2019, May 7). *Axolotl Life Cycle.* Lolly Brown. https://lollybrown.com/axolotl-life-cycle/

Clare, J. (2011b, December 1). *Axolotl Breeding*. Reptiles Magazine. https://reptilesmagazine.com/axolotl-breeding/

Clare, J. P. (n.d.). Axolotls - *Breeding Axolotls Successfully*. Www.axolotl.org. https://www.axolotl.org/breeding.htm

Georgia State University, & Young Harris College. (2022, March 3). *8 Fascinating Facts About The Axolotl*. Treehugger. https://www.treehugger.com/things-you-dont-know-about-axolotl-4863490

H, J. (2023, January 21). *5 Food Options For Axolotls*. PetHelpful. https://pethelpful.com/reptiles-amphibians/5-Food-Options-For-Axolotls

Hall, H. (2021, October 16). *Axolotl Lifespan: How Long Do They Live?* AZ Animals. https://a-z-animals.com/blog/axolotl-lifespan-how-long-do-they-live/#:~:text=Axolotls%20typically%20live%201 0%2D15

Hawk, T. (2022). *Axolotl For Beginners: 1x1 Guide For Species-Appropriate Keeping, Care And Feeding In The Aquarium Incl. Interesting Facts*. In Google Books. epubli. https://www.google.ae/books/edition/Axolotl_for_beginners/noRpEAAAQBAJ?hl=en&gbpv=1&dq=axolotls%20favorite%20foods&pg=PT17&printsec=frontcover

Majchrzak, A. (2020). *Ambystoma Mexicanum (Salamandra Ajolote)* (T. Dewey, Ed.). Animal Diversity Web. https://animaldiversity.org/accounts/Ambystoma_mexicanum/

San Diego Zoo Wildlife Alliance. (2019). *Axolotl* | San Diego Zoo Animals & Plants. Sandiegozoo.org. https://animals.sandiegozoo.org/animals/axolotl

Sunny. (2018, May 23). *Sick Axolotl, Fungus, Stress Symptoms [The Definitive Remedy Guide].* ExoPetGuides. https://exopetguides.com/axolotl/axolotl-symptoms-guide/

The Editors of Encyclopedia Britannica. (2017). *Axolotl | Amphibian.* In J. P. Rafferty (Ed.), Encyclopædia Britannica. https://www.britannica.com/animal/axolotl